HOW THE LEFT DESTROYED THE WESTERN NEGRO

In Memory of Tupac Shakur and
Malcolm X.
For the consciousness
and the courage.

HOW THE LEFT DESTROYED THE WESTERN NEGRO

INTRODUCTION

If the western world has inherited from the policies applied by the end of WWII between 1945 to 1947, it is more than important to specify that not much has changed since, especially when it comes to the political management of black peoples in the United States and Northerwestern Europe. Before we pursue this essay, it is necessary to specify which black category is involved in the socio-political context of the West. All Africans differ from one another for the continent is the place where one finds the most diverse phenotypes on earth. The black political context of the West is linked to history and therefore took a turn during slavery. The Blacks which will be mentioned in this study are of West African and Central Bantu origins and their descendants in the New World. They were at some point colonized by the French, the Belgians or the Brittons. Though their presence has been detected as early as the 15th century in the West, they have failed to achieve much sixty years after the decolonial movements. If other minorities such as the Vietnamese or Lao have, despite the great contempt they had to endure, managed to forge a strong political structure no matter where they migrated to, the Blacks have spent more time marching, dreaming, debating, asking, demanding, complaining more than working and creating a solid legacy. In this case, two communities will draw our attention: the

Afro-Americans and the Black French. By the end of the 1960s, both had the opportunity to stand up and build a valid political and economic entity. Yet, they would be guilty of going back to the state of mental slaves, hoping to find a new white savior who would speak out for them and lift them up. In both countries, the black man and woman has been infantilized to the maximum and was made as an incapable individual who can think for himself. Arrogant and reluctant to find their own solutions when other migrant groups did it, Blacks have been using the pain of the past faced by their forefathers to gain a privileged access to political power. In this quest, most of them forgot that the left, a paternalistic and colonial entity with a great disdain for any minority they manipulate to gain votes, only exploit them, their emotions and their rage to either create chaos, bring war or nurture tensions. Obsessed with the tragedy of the past, the western Negro wants the world to adapt to his own difficultie and always sides with white political agents which would encourage him not to face his own responsabilities. Evolving in a space where racism still exists, the black community had all the necessary tools to change their prospects and create a better place for their legacy. However, they failed by either becoming pure agents of capitalism or by engaging in the paternalistic schemes promoted by the leftist agents. Yet, even if the black individual sides with such powerful white entities, he will never hold the greatest privilege in their minds for other minorities will always come first before him. The Negro has become an emotional caricature used by various political powers to create a chaotic environement when times do not serve the political agenda of a given government. For this reason, the black community in the West has tremendously regressed and attributes such failures to systemic racism. In reality, their own racial obsession made them lazy enough to rebel, march and go back to their inner anger waiting for the next fight. Their own emotions have made them prisoners as they are now going in circle. For the most part, they have become more passive than active, blame others for their issues and are reluctant to build any structure, as they would attack and destroy, refuse to support the work of any black individual who would like to change the narrative by building a new structure which could benefit their own community. This study will focus on several points aimed to evoke the mental legacy left by the paternalistic leftist entity on the Negro mind and how, through arts, politics, sociology, such issues have contributed to the great regression of a people whose ancestors seemed to have a promising future in the sphere. In all the sections mentioned above, the blacks seem to always have one role: the passive agents.

BLACKS AND CAPITALISM

Black people in the west, whether in the United States or France can protest all they desire for equality but can not fool history. The new generation does not fight for truth and equality per se but now know how to exploit the political mechanisms and tactics to access power. Their fight is therefore not genuine, but calculated. And in this quest, the capitalization of black pain has become a standard. The Blacks do not constitute a better or more special community than any other one. They have been corrupted at heart by the improbable capitalistic machine through which anybody or any cause can be sold or bought in the quest of access to power.

In that effect, the political protests orchestrated by Black Americans in the summer of 2020 made no sense. The group in itself already has achieved the status of equality. They are now allowed to consume as they please. Yet, the exploitation of the pain of the past is a political action used as a tool to elevate their status to a higher special place. Blacks in the western sphere, especially African-Americans, have always wanted to show the world how the fight for equality was still important to them. Actually, they have betrayed the ideas of their forefathers in the 1960s, long ago and have now become no less different than any other opportunistic minority. Their protests are no longer authentic for nobody longs for being respected as a human being with dignity. The main interest of the black minority now is to access control. They understood the codes and political mechanisms which can allow them to be heard by the higher institutions. None among them truly wants to transmit or preserve the hard work of their elders. On the contrary, they would rather mimick them and wear their clothes as a pretense, a symbol of a deep black consciousness. In the western sphere of the 21st century, the hearts are politically corrupted and blacks would like to be treated differently when they too are no longer driven by an aspiration to freedom but by capitalism.

Such capitalistic approach can be seen in mainstream media. Blacks have proven to be prolific in debates, arguments and rebellion through the use of social media. In this specific case, the commentors or social media users use the pro-black arguments to nurture the angry emotions of a black passive population which has not been able to build anything over the past decades. Such tactics allow the black speaker to enjoy a status of preacher, or elevated individual who would have enough power to dominate over an audience. That fact would explain the great regression of the black western community. They would rather be obsessed with power and the domination of their own instead of rebuilding and moving forward equally with the other groups as one single nation. Most black people, it is true, love dreaming and hope to be carried away by figures they deem politically superior. Their sense of reality seems to be split and they are unable to understand the gravity of a given situation. If they blame racism for their lack of inclusion in their sphere, they forget to mention that many are still obsessed with trivial issues as the consumers they are and such obsession narrows their aspirations. The Eurocentric thesis in history are still being promoted by historians for a great lack of interest for the field by the black population as a whole. Other communities are present in higher fields of study such as archaeology, chemistry, biology or technology -the next war being centered on technology- but even there, black people are not numerous at all and only a few remain. Yet, this can not be an issue due to systemic poverty for, even in poverty, black women seem to be the highest consumers of goods but rather an issue which has to do with laziness and the constant desire of Blacks to get attention. The violence of their past was never meant to be exploited as a tool to dominate others but to help the other generations move forward and never forget. Yet, it is impossible for the black community to build any strong political structure for the members are not only too divided but also too scared to abandon their privileges and change their behavior. Anger allows them to get all the attention. While other groups such as the Persians, Indians or Chinese work in laboratories to develop the next gadget, Blacks still do not know how to evaluate power. They believe their domination should be centered around the money they generate, especially with music. In reality, as we will see in the next pages, they have been placed in a cycle from where they will not be able to escape.

In this sense, they are able to take a distance from the past, use it to their advantage so as to adjust the realities of their existence to their own black experience. They think about capitalism before black consciousness. Through their revolts they actually hope to insert black issues within the capitalistic sphere. In mercantilism, black issues and black pain should be perceived as an element which would grant them better privileges over other minorities. Blacks, whether in the United States or France, are not innocent and fear to no longer be treated as special. For this reason, they should not enjoy any special status of privilege and can not be perceived as the guardians of equality for they have, themselves, become extremely selective in terms of emotions. The recent protests in 2020 have highlighted a deep hatred of Blacks in the west for Donald Trump. Yet, if they accuse the latter to have been guilty of racism, the crimes committed by Barack Obama as well as his inability to improve the condition of Black Americans are still overlooked. Just like any other group in their sphere, Blacks loved Obama for his image and for the superficial symbol he embodied to their eyes. As a politically passive group which consumes more than its create, the Blacks considered Obama to have had a good influence upon their reality. Yet, though they pretend to be the sons of black rebels from the 60s, the new generation proved to be as cold and selective as the whites. Obama was one of the worst presidents ever who greatly contributed to the demise of Syria, Lebanon, and North Africa with the terrific Lybian issue. Yet, the destruction of a plurimillennial civilization such as Syria and the case of refugees tormented by the war never deterred the black community from supporting him throughout his eight years. Yet again, the recent political selection of Kamala Harris and Joe Biden, who had also been a great supporter of the war in Iraq in 2003, highlighted the contradiction of the said black community. Harris, an Indian woman with a little black heritage, was used, like Obama, as a tool by the left to seduce the black voters. Since the downfall of the Panthers, Black Americans have become extremely gullible and infantilized regarding their political choices. Their vote would be secure if the candidate is black or partially black as a guarantee of political efficiency. Yet, Harris has been guilty of having perpetuated mass incarceration of black men, married a white man, always claimed to be

Indian and not black and stated several times that she would never pass laws which would only benefit Blacks in the United States. Despite her great contempt for them, the Blacks still voted for her. This issue would take roots in colonialism itself and the state of dependency which characterizes most black communities. The left is a colonial entity in essence whose members, very paternalistic, hope to introduce themselves as the eternal guardians and guides of the Blacks. They are the good "Whites" who understand, support and fight for them. The 2020 protests have proven how Blacks truly need constant validation, attention. They have been made the colonial children of the left and refuse to take any responsabilities for their actions, hoping to always adapt and change the reality to their own. The white liberals are present to watch over them and silence any opponent which could be erased by the black agents formed by the white institutions themselves. The community is not looking for peace but has become arrogant and only wants to let its anger out and dominate out of rage. Through their failure to preserve the heritage of the Panthers, they proved to have been easily taken back by the system. Black Americans can not pretend to fight against the system. They have become the system.

***

Bi-partism has had a deep impact in the minds of millions of Blacks in the Western sphere. A symbol for the unique American political scene, it also nurtures and infantilize the minds by fueling a real dual vision of power. Politics is strangely perceived as a thing of the past or a science only made for the rich, the elite. Outside of the voting sessions which happen more or less every four years for many Western countries, the people often seem to be disconnected. The United States, masters of propaganda, have never ceased to promote such narrative to submit the citizens and control them. America was therefore introduced as the axis of good and the other non-white political leaders and their entities are deemed a threat and the "axis of evil". The same pathetic rhetoric has been spread within the various black communities of the Western sphere when it comes to the issue of "pro-blackness" and the protection of the black community. If such fight was crucial in the past, it has now become irrelevant for the original and authentic resistance in black liberation died in the late 1960s with the disappearence of African-American leaders. Our modern world was born in 1945 as leaders have worked to shift their political structure, from nation-state to a global and unique ideology and new world order. The recognition of slavery and the discussion on colonialism which took place over the past few years were a political strategy to fuel the anger and exploit the Blacks to start riots or further tensions within a given population. As global policies are taking place, most Blacks in the sphere are still trying to impose a political fight for black liberation with codes dating back to the 1960s, a time when Malcolm X was not exposed to the political ideologies of globalism as all he knew was the nation. Leftist and right-wing Blacks, either in the United States or France have engaged in a conflict which makes no sense at all in reality. Pro-blacks aim to maintain their authenticity and the black patriots integrate and have been accused of distancing themselves from their roots, as if blackness was to be accepted as an opposition to Europe. Slaves to their emotions, both parties refuse to take the new political structure into account. In the global political agenda, race is no longer important, as power only evolves around economic and financial domination. And in this case, both black parties have been guilty. In recent years, the fight for black liberation was proven to be rooted in mercantilism. The rise of social media has nurtured the expension of black egomaniacs in the making who understood the mechanisms needed to make profit off of black pain. The far right Blacks have been using the same methods too. None of them could claim authenticity when, in essence, they are no longer oppressed Africans who struggle to be embraced as full human beings, but black people in color who have tremendously accepted the brutal mechanisms of mercantilism with the hope to, not only dominate their own kind, but achieve power as well. They have prostituted their essence for consumerism. Blacks want to be perceived as the guardians of morals, as if the pain of their ancestors could give them the right to be seen as eternal victims who would be good and kind in the heart. In their scheme, white institutions have to be the eternal face of brutality and domination. Life in the western sphere showed otherwise. Black people themselves can be the oppressors of their own and such behavior have a direct or indirect impact in Africa itself as well. Millions of them have paid expensive phones or high technology objects produced by global companies whose leaders and founders were found guilty of exploiting the natural resources of the continent. Black people in the western sphere have always failed to distance themselves from capitalism and marketing. This obsession for money is the consequence of a trauma which first began during the slave trade. At that time, Blacks were exposed to the first experimentations of mass capitalism. Yet, the enslaved Africans were never given the chance to experiment the joy of buying, selling and owning and thus of possessing. By the late 1960s, most Black Panthers and African-American leaders have been overthrown or exiled. A few years later, the United States government found the perfect way to tarnish and annihilate the legacy of the black leaders by exposing Black Americans to the freedom of capitalism and mass consumerism, either financially or sexually. At the time, during the Cold War, the American government had the strong desire to nurture the American Dream and send a strong message to the USSR. The United States had to be this rainbow nation where any body could succeed through a constant reinvention in culture and politics. Such propaganda would allow African-Americans to openly access the status of millionaire. By the 1980s, a group of Black Americans, who were despised a few years ago, can freely buy, possess and own, a privilege they had been deprived of for centuries.The Black Panthers and other leaders such as Malcolm X or Martin Luther King had the same desire. They fought for the dignity of Black people, yes, but most of all, they wanted them to be recognised as simple human beings who deserved to be treated with respect first of all. The emphasis was put on the mental, on the essence of Black people not on their exploitation through money. Yet, the expansion of mass consumerism promoted by the US government and introduced to Black Americans have sent them back to their first place. They would no longer be embraced through their spirit but appreciated through their bodies, a situation similar to that of slavery. If Black Americans are scared to disappear, money and consumerism would maintain their status. In reality, they have regressed and failed miserably as they are now capitalizing off their own dehumanization which dates back to slavery. Modern black women, deeply impacted by western feminism, have now come back to the sex slave status which was imposed onto them when their first female ancestors were kidnapped and deported to America. Their black leaders are now entertainers, hence, agents of excessive mercantilism. The women have been way more sexualized than before as more and more female artists boast about their private parts or sexual prowess. Such narrative is not only destructive but also an insult to the Black victims of rape during slavery. Mercantilism has now become the rampart to the ideas promoted by the Black Panthers who mostly focused on the intellectual expansion of their minds, disgusted by the exploitation of their bodies. Black Americans have not only betrayed the fight of their predecessors but they did even worst as they let their institutions use them as the principal targets to introduce destructive political agendas so as to tarnish the Western environement. Few other communities capitalize off of their sexual attributes to sell more profit. If the African American community seemed to be prosperous in the 1960s with the birth of bright black leaders, it is now clear to assert that they have now failed their mission. The black community in the United States has been massively exposed to the other Blacks in

Europe, who identified to them for lack of representation in their respective European country, for their incredible musical talent, the grace of their older entertainers such as Whitney Houston for instance, yet, such community was never the best in the American sphere. European Blacks were impacted by them as they were apart of the most powerful nation on earth, the United States. The African populations in the Caribbean or in Peru or Colombia are as talented as the Black Americans. Yet, their nations are deprived of the same power and therefore, their impact has been tremendously reduced. Today, most Black American artists are the first to promote repulsive messages. Black women have now fully embraced the sex slave status slave masters had promoted a few centuries prior, and use their sex drive to promote and sell. The American institutions have succeeded in using them as the face of decay when black leaders in the 1960s fought to focus on the elevation of the minds. The African-Americans are not free at all. They are mentally enslaved to money, obsessed with power and have a dysfunctional vision and relationship to it. They have a fear of losing, when already lost, and wrongly believe that the lack of possession would lead them to their decay when their institutions have made them the new face of decay. The American domination and our own sensitivity and lack of self-esteem did encourage us to worship and emulate the style and culture of a group which proved to be more dysfunctional than one thinks. The decay also favored a great infantilization of the minds among the African American women as well. Many, when exposed to politics, lack logic and are driven by their ethnic emotions, even when the black candidates introduced to them have openly proven to be anti-black, having a huge disdain for a community they deem low. American politics proved many times how Black women would be the first to vote for the political party they deem to be led by nice white people. The violence of their past have not only crushed them but worst, it favored a suspension in their quest of appreciation by white people. Despite it all, as they enjoy the privilege to be apart of the most powerful nation in the world, they are no longer able to exist without the approval and recognition of the White party they vote for.

The new generation of Black Americans have strongly regressed as they exported the politics of color. Any Black or mixed-race candidate would be automatically embraced, loved and cherished by the black community, even when such candidate had passed laws or said words which aimed to hurt and damage black men and women. The infantilization relies on the obsession of skin color. Being Black seems to be perceived as an instant proof of validation, even when it is not. This would be a proof of solidarity and self-love, even when such candidate has always been destructive and evil. It is now more than accurate to admit that capitalism has damaged and annihilated a whole community which is now gone as no other bright political leader similar to Malcolm X could exist today. Yet, though they betrayed the essence of the Black Panthers, many Black Americans want to mimick the authenticity of the leaders in the 1960s. It is more than common to notice groups promoting mass consumerism, all the while trying to emulate the depth of the Black Panthers when the core of their revolt is already tarnished. Capitalism has allowed younger black generations to buy and exploit the struggle of their elders. A fact which allows them to further their different forms in terms of financial and sexual consumption. The Black Panthers were not only political but their social work for their people was a threat. They organized to educate, feed and elevate their own kind and did not need any form of approval from the Whites. The emergence of Malcolm X at the time was problematic too for the White institutions. *Black Lives Matter* was fabricated and never sincere. Financed by various organizations owned by the Clintons, among others, they were the symbol of the Black American failure. As the majority of their former leaders were either killed, exiled or died of natural causes, the rich intellectual African-American culture has been totally tarnished by the new leaders of such community. Indeed, the new faces of black power and people are not writers, authors, publishers or politicians but singers, entertainers, rappers and dancers. Introduced as models of success, they were placed as "new leaders" as a mockery from the white institutions. Celebrities will forever be at the bottom of the ladder of success and political influence. Money will never replace one's social status. Most African American celebrities were never born into money and hope to be new bourgeois when they do not understand the codes. A singer would be an influencer for basic individuals who failed to invest in their lives, not seeing any particular talent in themselves. The entertainer in himself, though rich, is a miserable failure for paid to entertain and to lie, their power relying on fools with no concept of self-esteem. Hence, he is not a politician.

In our global sphere of today, the most powerful entity is the one which funds. The director or CEO of one company has no power unless he funds it himself. The entertainer is a slave to the industry as well as to various white men who have funded corporations and imposed their schemes, tactics and rules upon singers, dancers or actors who, have no other choice but to submit to the machine. The likes of performers such as Beyoncé or her husband Jay-Z are a good example. Promoted by the media as leaders of their community, the individuals they dominate have elevated them to the status of gods. Black people love to worship others for they were never taught to conquer and own since the times of slavery which made them passive beings. For this reason, many young Blacks have a high propensity for dreaming and projecting their own desires through the lives of others. Such demise distort their vision. A prize given to a black singer makes such artist a world influencer and a political figure even when the same artist promotes wrong ideologies which destroy his brothers and sisters. Most Blacks in the western sphere are guilty of not capturing the spirit of economics at all. Few understand the mechanisms which lie behind it. None of these Black American celebrities who have been promoted to their peers own, possess or fund. They have the money, yet, they are owned. Their bodies, hair, weight, skin color do not even belong to them but are owned by beauty company representatives with whom they signed contracts to extend their worldwide visibility. The men of the shadows ruling the industry are the ones in charge, not the artists. The white American political institutions know well about the infantilization of the minds in the black community and their strong desire to dream for they ignore how to conquer. Placing the entertainers as leaders is a great mark of disdain from the latter party, a sign which contribute to the mental and psychological decay of the African-Americans. The promotion of entertainers is a message to the Blacks in the United States. To the eyes of the White institutions, Black Americans have to be maintained to the lower sphere. Their only power can be accessed through singing, dancing, the sexualization of the self and the promotion of gullible agenda not the elevation of the minds or mental stimulation. A performer is an entertainer of the fools, a tool used to promote diversion of the mass.

WESTERN BLACKS AND ENTERTAINMENT

Blacks in the Western sphere have always failed to understand and measure the different scales which constitute the functionality of power. So far, since the destruction of the Black Panthers, entertainment has been the only channel through which a black domination was accepted. There again, most artists compose, write, exploit their own bodies but do not own any particular structure. If the Black Panthers have attempted to encourage the Black Americans to own and be the leaders of their future, consumerism has had a destructive impact on Blacks. They have become extremely passive as they consider their right to consume and buy excessively as a new door to freedom. From this, the institutions have not only infantilized them with the manichaen political vision of events, they also favored the obsession of the factor color, the obsession of being accepted by the white institutions and the projection of their lives through entertainment. Over the decades, African descendants in both Europe and the United States have relied on the actions of black entertainers. They would be deemed an example for their wealth, their ability to tour and the numbers of followers and records sold around the world. A person with no knowledge and understanding of power would only fall over such facts for many in the elite, who value the different ladders of power, know that entertainers, whether singers, actors or models will forever be at the bottom. They are the entertainers of the fools. For this reason, a few actors, whether white or black, try to step away from their craft to join politicians so as to elevate their status, being aware that outside of the mass, an entertainer exists to divert people and lie to passive individuals. However, due to their deep infantilization and lack of independence, Africans consider their favorite artists to be really powerful. Artists, especially when black, do not belong to themselves at all but to corporations whose members exploit them, take advantage of them to make profit. In some cases, some black female singers sign contract with beauty companies and are forbidden to cut their hair or modify their bodies which are insured. The money earned is just an illusion and can not be valued of respected. The entertainer is nothing less than a new slave to the market and trends, a product made to be crafted to generate millions. Yet, the racist institutions have so much disdain for the blacks that they would endlessly promote their favorite singers as examples of success. Such issue would, furthermore, signify that a black child could only hope to succeed by becoming a singer or an actor and that. Through this, an entire generation of black children have wrongly thought to follow the easy path and abandon intellectual and scientific matters to earn fast money. The treatment of celebrities by the Hollywood machine shows, on the contrary, that there is no value attributed to them. Recently, black entertainers in the United States have successfully exploited the trauma surrounding police brutality. They not only promote the excessive propaganda of raw capitalism which destroyed the Black community feminism being one cause for women are good consumers in the sphere- but attempt to play both sides by claiming to be conscious of their heritage. Therefore, Blacks have spent more time projecting their experience through other artists instead of truly working on themselves. The black entertainer is not only a manipulator, but a good supplier to the white savior complex as well. Due to the years of infantilization, Africans in the United States and Western Europe have been waiting for a savior who would change their lives. They are disconnected and reluctant to either question themselves or work to achieve greater things. Money has become their only value and not work per se. The entertainer could be compared to the effects of the Evangelical Church in the nurturing of passivity. Blacks have a mechanism within them which is easily manipulated by foreign forces. The origins are overlooked and they privilege emotivity at the expense of the facts.

ON THE IMPROBABLE NATURE OF OPPOSING BLACKS AND WHITES: A EUROPEAN CONTEXT

Over the years, the European minorities were deeply affected, when it comes to the politics of self-affirmation, by the evil effects of a Black American influence. If the younger generations, and rightfully so, hope to decolonize the minds and repair the wounds inflicted upon the families by treating issues such as colorism, racism, self-hatred or by the creation of space for our own kind, we have mostly failed, depending on the European countries we come from, to favor our own ways of thinking and politics as well. First of all, the black individual suffers from a deep emotional issue. The isolation, rejection and social injustice experienced led many of us to become easily manipulated by other white entities, political parties whose members hoped to defend us, while we should have been able to figure it out on our own. Blacks have been, for almost fifty years the perfect useful allies to leftist parties whose politicians relentlessly used their pain, and suffering to advance their own causes. They not only abused them and made a mockery of their inner struggles, they also never gave them the sacred space they promised as they shamelessly downgraded their value by comparing their unique experience to other groups perceived as minorities too. Since the 1970s, the minorities have been the perfect allies needed, the pawns which needed to be thrown at their opponents in the right field. We have witnessed how the minorities elected by the left were always used as agents to destroy and turn the politics to their advantage. They have destroyed the black communities more than they have freed them. The manipulation of black minds relics on the constant reminder of black misery: slavery, colonialism, forced displacement, evictions, poverty, isolation or even police brutality. These helped black people evolve with a spirit of anger towards the white institutions without even understanding that they had been taken advantage of. Since the colonial era, each and every Black European, to different degree, hopes to be validated by the white entities which govern them. This stems from the past, a cruel time when our very essence could not be embraced or accepted without the approval of our "masters". This feeling did nurture the infantilization which prevents us from thinking rationally and logically. As Western Europe has been conquered and culturally colonized by the great American power, the minorities were, without even noticing it, impacted by the dysfunctional thoughts of such politics. It is true that the right- wing parties have betrayed the essence of their deep essence to submit their nations to corporations, the European Union and the United States, and the left has nurtured the brutal racial policies by importing them from the United States to us. In reality, both parties, both political parties, or ideologies, behaved like colonial entities for us and prevented a great number of our brothers and sisters to successfully implant themselves in the nations their ancestors had migrated to. Despite racism and xenophobia, a great implantation was possible. Western Europe, though sometimes backwards in terms of social progress, gave Blacks the space to build and create a good economic platform for their kind. They mostly wrongly thought that relying on leftist parties, or good "white people" would have helped them in their demise when the greatest solution should have come from a huge display of solidarity, the building of different companies, the valuation of entrepreneurship, the perfect balance between their respective cultures and European cultures, the acceptance that they belong to a middle ground and financial prosperity. The pain and suffering of our parents and forefathers should have been a motivating factor to encourage them to work even harder. Yet, blinded by their emotions, they followed the words of political parties which hijacked them from implanting our their economy in their respective European nations. In reality, the black European experience could have never been compared to that of the African-Americans. Indeed, the European structure greatly differs from that of the United States. For this reason, many organizations financed by the Left want to import the brutality of the Black American experience in Europe so as to advance their own political agenda. Victims and prisoners of our own emotional feelings, we are easily trapped into believing in a common white enemy when, such reasoning is now obsolete. In the 21st century, one can not think of White and Black as the opposition now turns around the global powers and forces and the sovereignty of the people. The financial crisis of 2008, followed by the economic failure caused by the COVID 19 accentuated such truth. The global forces of the 21st century have crushed businesses and lives without distinguishing races. In the European context, thinking about whiteness and blackness and opposing them in these times when the world has shifted to a brutal global dictatorship is adding fuel to the fire and affects people more than before. Most Blacks are guilty to believe that the power of Brussels only affects white people and not them. Yet, as long as African descendants live and breath here, they will be the victims of colonial policies imposed by Brussels and the European Union. Western European politics has now become an attack on our freedom and the militarization of our societies have accentuated the brutal character of such global forces. Yet, blinded by their own anger and violence for the pain of their forefathers, people fail to envision such great danger before our eyes. The incapacity of many to see the global shift in European politics will disappoint, as most of us will, in the future, feel used by the same parties whose members claimed they would help us. The issue is no longer about race or minorities but globalism and its effects. Colonialism is now displayed between banks, corporations and the people. We, even if we do not want it, are also a part of the people.

COLOR VS NATIONS

It is no secret. The world has now evolved towards a new order we never saw before. The nation-state is in danger and being challenged by foreign forces. Throughout the many protests of 2020, one thing can be asserted. Nothing said by black European activists, who heavily copy African-Americans in the matter, can be trusted. They are agents nurtured by opponent white political forces whose main goal is to overthrow and create confusion. They want to oppose the color against the nation. As we will see it later with the case of the Black African French, one individual can not survive without one or several identities, customs and regulations. The skin color can be an indication of the origins of one individual, yet it can not define social structure. The Black French have become a living failure for this reason. Manipulated by the *Parti Socialiste* since 1981 and encouraged by their immigrant allies, the population is now confused. After years of orchestrated mutiny, the Black French Africans believe that embracing their French heritage is an absolute disgrace towards their African heritage. The Black activists want French culture gone, and would like to replace it with the skin color factor. They deem the French culture racist and incompatible with their blackness. Ignorant, many forget that France, though racist in its institutions, was always more progressive and contradictory than any other Western European state at the time. The presence of Blacks in Europe is not recent and dates back to thousands of years earlier. The Black French activists want one to believe that the nation will crush the color arguing that the institutions are racist. Yet, it is a lie. The institutions are one group and the people governed by these institutions are another one. The White French people, though guilty of preserving silly prejudices against immigrants, are arrogant and too proud. Yet, they are not hateful. However, the constant pressure imposed upon them by Black French activists is a danger which will eventually push a whole generation of White French to organize in gangs to attack the descendants of immigrants in the streets of Paris. Mixing the institutions with the people is a danger in itself. French culture is rich. Not in the music industry, for many French performers have proven not to be good vocalists at all, but in the realm of cuisine, movies, fashion and better, in literature. This cultural wealth and beauty is being attacked by colorist individuals who aim to destroy it. One never asked the descendants of immigrants to deny their ancestry, but their integration would have been a success if they had understood that exchanging one's African culture for the French culture was not an act of self-hatred but pure logic which would have prevented the loss of identity. French literature is rich enough for people of color to feel connected. Many Black West Indian authors such as Alexandre Dumas, Aimé Césaire, Frantz Fanon or even Maryse Condé have left a tremendous legacy writing about the black experience in one way or another. France was never the horrific country black activists want you to think it is. How many African-American writers left the

American Segregation to live in France in the late 19th century and early 20th? Most of them remained there and claimed that the treatment they received in France could not be compared to the one in the United States. However, none of these positive factors are mentioned by these dangerous political activists. The majority are nothing less than egomaniacs in the making who center their political ideologies around themselves. Their inner anger and thirst for domination push them to attack any individual who does not think alike. The French culture could have become a culture of substitution for millions of African French who would have found a sense of belonging as the Black Europeans have always been here. In this equation, exchanging the lost African culture for the French culture is fair. Yet, preserving the color factor, with a lost African culture and asking to overthrow the French institutions so as to fight against racism makes no sense.

ON IDENTITY

As I am writing now, Western Europe has been plagued by the sudden presence of a deadly virus. The Nations, led by the political colonial entity known as the European Union, have entered a new phase in the management of the crisis. With the use of the police, the populations have been forced to close their businesses, now victims of an uncertain future. The world has now changed from the nation-state to a global village. Events are coordinated and any decision taken by one regional leader affects the neighboring countries. Since the 2008 election of Barack Obama, the entire world has been used to the effects of synchronicity. The use of social media, supported by the development of technology have easily led us to the submission of such upheaval. The world has swifted. The year 2020 has been crucial as many secret black organizations, supported by foreign parties, had been financed and sent out to disrupt the western structures. If the murder of George Floyd could have been used as a new way to open up to each other and debate when it comes to the place of Blackness in the western world, it did not change anything for us. They destroyed more than they built. Worst, the protests revealed that the black populations in the Great West have never evolved over the years or changed their narrative. They are still the great victims of oppression and never question their own responsabilities. The 2018 unnoticed lynching of Loic Kamtchouang in the streets of Paris in the summer of 2018 is a proof of that. A homeless 23 year old French-Cameroonian, he was a stranger to the gangster life and was brutally lynched by ten other Black kids. Not one single French-African political or public figure spoke out to denounce the violence in the ghettos. Indeed, in this capitalistic society, one sells and buys to make himself heard. And the marketing of black rage and pain is no more different at all. The protests led by so-called black French leaders in June of 2020 allowed them to change the narrative and omit their part of responsability in their inability to build anything. The French-African experience needs to be talked about as it is one of the most tragic in Western Europe. Actually, the French West Indians already did the intellectual work to advance their situation. Yet, no one can say the same when it comes to the African immigrants and their descendants. Out of all the Africans present in Western Europe, the French-Africans had the best opportunities to succeed and change for the better. The Black Portuguese do not exist in Portugal and are even pushed aside geographically, forced to live outside of the capital and evolve in silence. They are treated like subhuman individuals and have to deal with the worst kind of police and state abuses. The case of Elson Sanches, who was shot point blank at the age of 14 by a corrupt white Portuguese policeman illustrates our point. Since his murder in 2009, the policeman was acquitted and still walks free. The Black French had the chance to evolve in a space where there was already a certain Black visibility, thanks to the presence of the Black West Indians or *Antillais*. Though filled with prejudices, the White French individual is not a hateful man. The real danger and racism in France are the institutions, not the population. The institutions are those which block and break the black body and mind, not the people. Therefore, the French-Africans had the possibility to walk into the way paved by the Black West Indians to build their own structure and become fully integrated. If many claim rejection and racism as a reason for their distanciation towards the French identity and citizenship, it is important to recall the truth. The French-African is not independent in the mind and still wants to be approved and recognised by the White governing entity. This mentality dates back to colonialism as the French settlers brainwashed their subjects, manipulating them to a point where they would worship them and hope to be a part of them. The white authorities have thus abandoned them to a cynical form of suspension ever since. And this absence of recognition breaks the mind of the French-African. He has proven to be unable to build, unable to embrace his own identity and is filled with sadness as the white entity refuses to give him what he wants. The French-African immigrant experience is a tragedy as their chances were hijacked by the *Parti Socialiste* whose members used them to consolidate their place. Since the election of 1981, and the appointment of François Mittérand, France saw the first emergence of anti-racist institutions and associations made to help and assist the North and West African immigrant in the 1980s. Without realizing it, still saddened by the rejection of the right wing

70

parties which never thought of them as real French citizens, one entire generation of Black immigrants fell for the imperialistic leftist ideologies. The *Parti Socialiste* was made to be the friend of these Black people. For the first time, the French-African found an ally, and felt happiness in his heart as he was being recognised and embraced. This friendship and understanding of the *Parti Socialiste* towards the Blacks was never genuine but it was pure colonial imperialism. The Socialists never considered the immigrants as equals but needed their trust to use them against their right-wing enemies. Since the 1980s, the black immigrants have become the pawns used by different social movements to attack the conservatists. The emotivity of the French-Africans unabled one entired generation to become stable Black French. The politics of victimization and blame made them waste a lot of time and they eventually failed their success. The racist French institution had carefully put an end to the intellectual West African immigration from the 1940s until 1960s replacing them by African workers deprived of any knowledge when it comes to social status. It was impossible for the White goverment to have future Black intellectual children who would have represented a threat to the White French children. The sons of the black factory workers were already broken and deprived of any African identity before they were even born.

They saw the light in France, not really understanding why their families had emigrated. The interference of the *Parti Socialiste* nurtured a feeling of pride characterized by their inability to form a coherent political structure for their own. Until this day, the French-African is void and unaware of his identity. He has not built, is scared and has the audacity to demand and request loudly when he has never proven anything to society. There was no way for these French-African immigrants to evolve outside of a full integration to France. Their parents were the product of a failure, symbolized by the waves of independance. They never possessed and were the products of chaos and destruction.

Their arrival in France sealed the deal. It is important to acknowledge that the French-Africans never brought anything to French culture. They would have added a twist had they fully integrated and become Black French citizens. Improbable panafrican leaders have been so adament while trying to prove how Blackness and French identity could not go hand in hand at all, when according to history, even before Slavery, Africans have always been in Europe. The pro-Black and failed leaders never left Europe themselves, too busy with their privileges and consumerism. They used the argument of neo-colonialism to prevent any Black African immigrant from feeling French when the government and the people are two separate things. There was no way the immigrants could have brought a novelty within the land of their former colonial entity as they were already broken upon arriving there. Their parents were African and Black, yes, but they already lost their culture and heritage and never transmitted it to the fullest. The issue never had anything to do with color or race but with culture which the immigrants lacked. It would have been better for these African immigrants, with whom the possibility to build anew was vain due to their background, to exchange their lost African culture for the French one. That one, when it comes to literature, music, cinema or other had nothing to do with the despicable acts committed by the colonial entities. Had they become Black French citizens, despite the rejection of some, they would have become a stable community and the best example of integration, mental and financial success among the Western Blacks. Yet, it did not happen and France is a prison of the monsters they created. The years of resentment fueled by the *Socialiste* power have highlighted the points of one brutal social crisis. Now the black immigrants have become arrogant and more demanding than ever. None of them want to build but destroy and dominate, though blind and without a plan. No one cares about the ideas promoted by the oppressive *Hoteps*. We accept the separation and division. Some will never want to form a black

European coallition and we can not convince anybody. The situation is dangerous and we have wasted enough time complaining without building. This structure shall be built without any individual who is used to waste time. The other Black Europeans, should not end up like the Black French as many other alternatives can exist to share our own voice without the interference of other parties, whether Black or White. We shall not beg to exist, but organize to protect the double heritage we were born in and the importance we represent in history. As Western European countries are crumbling down, bought back by corporations, as the White populations deny their customs and ancestry replacing them by uber consumerism, our heritage, experience and identities are threatened too. We represent the middle, the end of a past which needs to be told and preserved. We may vary through our racial make ups, with our Nations, some of us being Belgians, Swedes, British, or even Germans but we need to gather and repair what we can do for us and our advancement, politically and socially. It is time to fully embrace the category we embody. Black Europeans are not Black Americans and shall never aspire to be. The African-Americans have failed miserably in protecting the ideologies of the Black Panthers by selling themselves to capitalistic ideas which destroyed their community more than anything else. We are not the same. Though we share our respect and admiration, it is safe to say that the younger generations, beginning in the early 1980s, tarnished the legacy of their forefathers and mothers. Black Europeans could become the next most powerful Black group in the Western sphere, especially when the United States are slowly declining from inner powers which attack one another. As we mentioned it earlier, the *socialiste* entities, as well as shady far right movements, want to use us as pawns to attack their opponents to later abandon us to our fate. In this violent period, it is more than important to remain careful and reject any provoked excitement made to blur our vision. Duality killed a generation of African parents and also contributed to the issue their children are now facing. The goal is not to hate white people or attack them. One should learn how to live with independence, never leaning on them to appreciate himself. Only weak Blacks will remain in this old scheme. One fights the institution with the endless building of structures and economic domination. After years of humiliation, many African parents turned to the colonial tactics of elitism to secure the future of their children. This favored a deeper distance between the poorest populations and the wealthiest ones. This division actually bothers us more than it elevates us. The poorest need the help of the richest and vice versa. The toxicity of blackness politics only stems from panafricanism, an anticolonial movement which centers blackness through the colonial gaze of the Western and Bantu descendants of the continent. Just like panarabism has confused and reduced the great perspectives of many "Arabized" populations in the East, panafricanism concluded that blackness could only be contemplated through the lens of West and Central African cultures, within the fake national borders created by evil and cruel white entities. Such vision opposes the legacy of black people in ancient Rome or Greece. Indeed, if their existence has now been fully recognised, Blackness or la *Négritude* was never restricted to West or Central Africa. Blackness could also be built in spaces deemed "White" or "European". The ancestors were free to travel beyond the very limits of the African continent. They would rather occupy lands and spaces rather than stop when a limit was drawn. Such vision only dates back to the European slave trade and colonialism. For this reason, it was wrongly thought that embracing blackness was opposed to accepting one's European identity as well, when the African ancestors proved that such idea was more normal than anything else. If right-wing parties isolated minorities, and now have to deal with the consequences of the anger they have nourished, we excluded ourselves even more for no reason when all we had to do was embrace, buy, build and gather to become the most important Black union ever. We complained more than we organized and united with one another. It was possible to keep and respect both cultures as well. Yet, our egos would never let us do. As we suffered from isolation, Black European leaders, or I should say, improvised black leaders, always proved to be failures to their community. Impacted by the brutal policy of capitalism, these so-called leaders have learnt the mechanisms of racial marketing, the exploitation of the pain, suffering of their community to position themselves as supreme leaders. Assa Traoré in France is one example. Manipulated and used by different leftist groups, she has been guilty of manipulating the public opinion to advance her own goals. Though the first in line to defend her brother, she never used her platform to talk about a bigger issue in the French ghettos, such as the rampant violent cases of murders among young Black boys. The case of Loic Kamtchouang, a French-Cameroonian homeless boy of 23, savagely lynched in 2018, was never evoked or mentioned by Traoré who does not seem any financial gain in speaking on such issues. Black European leaders, like African leaders, can not be trusted and are the enemies of the people. They take more than they build. In reality, Blacks need to be more mature, decolonize their minds and put an end to the endless desire to rely on a third party which would free them, whether through religion or famous figures -hence politics. The first decolonial action a

Black person can do is fight against the spirit of infantilization which tortures him. The Black European leaders not only copy and plagiarize the works of African-Americans, they also hope to place themselves at the top of the pyramid and govern a lost people who do not even understand their importance in such region of the world. Actually, Black French embody such a chaotic structure which needs to be mentioned. There, the political reflection and thoughts of black people has been belittled to the maximum. If not being entertained by the American life displayed on social media, they solely focus on the color factor, embracing any individual who happens to be Black, without even looking into the agenda. Such reflection also stems from the failure of African-Americans. Even if the honorable Black Panthers and Malcolm X expressed deep feelings concerning their community, the Black Americans in the 21st century have certainly regressed and their actions prove to be worst than before. If these black leaders were supposed to represent independence and an alternative to integration, they failed in everything. They proved that Blacks should have been integrated to European culture as "independence" prevent them from evolving. Their idea of independence is just another form of slavery. A slavery to the ego and the obsession with domination and power to crush other Blacks. If we hope to shift our political impact before it is too late, then, we have no other choice but to distance ourselves from the various influences which have been imposed onto us for many years so as to focus on our own heritage and issues. We are not Americans but Europeans of African descent, with our own roots and perspectives. They need to be valued too.

ON THE FRENCH DOWNFALL AND GLOBALISM

France will fall back to the 15th mondial rank of global powers due to the extreme racism and narrow-minded spirit of the members of its institutions. Actually, it is safe to acknowledge that the majority of sons and daughters of immigrants do not even understand the nature of

French racism. If most of them complain about rejection, they have failed to fathom that the French population is guiltier of nurturing prejudices than being hateful per se. For this reason, their obsession for protests will never allow them to move out of their vicious circle they have created themselves. In France, one's success always depends on the approval of the higher members of any given institution or hierarchy and such schemes apply to any sphere, from the lowest to the highest. Freemasonry, it is true, is the real hidden power of the French political structure yet whether in music, cinema, or arts in general, France hates the new and likes to rely on the old. Media, whether political or musical have been controlled by the same *connaisseurs*. Even the lowest structures such as *Le Mouv* or *Skyrock* whose journalists focus on French hip-hop are reluctant to allow Black French authors regarding the topic of colonialism in music to be promoted on their platforms, when it is the lowest sphere ever. The knowledge needs to come from white people first and if Blacks are encouraged to create they are isolated and ignored if they hope to theorize anything. On the cultural level, France is the only country where a one-hit wonder from the 1980s or 1990s can hope to tour, earn money, sign deals and be invited to every musical TV show from the public service as an homage to that one single time his own creation made people dream and feel better about themselves. If one-hit wonders deal with the utmost lack of respect for their inability to have reinvented themselves over the years in the UK or the United States, France loves to rely on self-sufficiency and their worshipping of the past. Unfortunately, such issue reflected in their politics too.

France was always a victim of its Latin spirit. For this reason it is reluctant to social and political change. The arrival of immigrants in the 1970s was perceived as a threat for not only the preservation of the French race but also to politics when, in reality, many modern issues would have been avoided if the institutions had automatically included them as full French citizens fifty years ago. If so, these North African and West African immigrants would have been, today, the first defenders of the nation. On the contrary, they have now become the enemies from within whose descendants will attack the structures from the inside. Latin countries such as France, Portugal or Spain, which have had colonies in Africa and in the Americas, tend to center their power around their institutions. It comes from them and is approved by them. Most members of such institutions are aged masons disconnected from the reality of the world who rely on the perpetuation of old codes which fell into oblivion ages ago. Northern European institutions are as racist as the French ones, yet the mentality is not the same at all. Not one single racist white British would deny that a Jamaican-British is a British citizen. The British have surpassed the racial and color factor years ago and always retributed people according to their own abilities. Contrary to France, the UK, Canada or the United States do not hide their true motives behind a hypocrite veil. They do create socioethnic data and are not afraid to talk about race unlike the French who hope to hide their true motives behind the creation of a false equal rainbow-like nation which is far from existing. The Northern Europeans are not afraid to speak about their true desire to maintain their global influence and power and even if the world changes tomorrow, as we are facing a new multipolar structure, the UK will always be respected by the other nations and will carry its power. These nations have been able to remain at the top for their unshameful desire to apply efficient selectivity regarding immigrant policies. The institutions in France do not want to evolve, but hope to keep the power to themselves first. And the domination of Canada, the United

States, the UK or the Dutch speaking part of Belgium can clearly be explained by their selectivity towards immigrants. The institutions of these countries understood that the inclusion of the best immigrants would not only contribute to the African brain drain, a fact which allows them to maintain their position over the continent, but also contribute to their political and academic elevation. In the world classment of colleges, the best European universities chosen are from the UK and from the Dutch speaking part of Belgium such as the Leuven institution. French universities do not belong. The UK has often recognised the diplomas of Nigerian, Ghanian or Indian students who have been formed academically in their original countries. Such factor not only adds more value to the competence of the previously mentioned African and Asian universities but also helps maintain the kingdom at the top.

However, France has failed miserably on this aspect and the institutions are now paying the price for their improbable political tactics. Contrary to popular belief, France had an African elite between the 1940s and 1960s. Yet, the existence of Senegalese, Togolese or Malian intellectuals during the process of decolonization was perceived as a danger. Indeed, these African men were not workers but thinkers, authors, journalists and from them, a new generation of leaders could overthrow the French power. The institutions were scared they would organize politically. Worst, the children of these Africans would be educated as well and they would constitute a deep threat to the other white children members of the elite. For this reason, the institutions have often been reluctant to grant scolarships and citizenships to African students after the 1960s independence and would replace them by the immigration of African workers from North, West and failed intellectuals from Congo-Brazzaville and Gabon. The workers mostly came from the poorest districts of African capitals with poor value of social classes. They would be exploited, sent to live in the ghettos and, except for some ethnic groups such as the Hausa, Soninke or Fulani who already had a great culture of trading, most of them were guilty to be dependent and unable to create their own structures. Their children would grow up between the walls of their ghettos and the old culture of their parents. By allowing these workers to come, the French institutions knew they would succeed in slowing down their pace of evolution. As dependent as they were, they knew most would never have the courage to build for themselves, be entrepreneurs but would end up relying on the state for financement and by procreating a lot. Work would therefore not be valued anymore. The Congo-*Brazzavillois* and the Gabonese would be too arrogant to walk away from their intellectual status and obsessed with being embraced and recognised by the white French elite they never had any spirit of giving back value to their fellow African immigrants believing they were superior to them in many ways. The exploitation of the workers and the rejection of the 1950s intellectuals was also a way for France to keep their influence in Africa. Without neocolonialism in West and Central Africa, France would belong to the 25th rank. The orchestrated military coups in Burkina-Faso or Ivory Coast allowed them to maintain such influence along with the help of their corrupted agents in Congo-Brazzaville and Gabon. Now that the country is going through the 2020 wordwide pandemic, inner conflicts have erupted. The isolated poor immigrants from the ghetto have been efficently manipulated for almost forty years and now carry a deep hatred for France. Arrogant, they hope to change the environment to their advantage. As they lack unity, they have mostly been unable to create their own socio-economic structures as well for too obsessed with victimhood, when other minorities such as the Lao or Vietnamese which had suffered the same fate and for whom integration was a success. When it comes to the question of immigration, France now pays for its inability to pass forward the race question. Though Black people have always been present in the country for more than centuries before slavery, most fail to recognise descendants of immigrants as French. Yet, are the immigrants the only ones to blame? Actually, the attitude of the immigrants, sons and daughters of former French colonies, reflect that of the white French themselves. Both entities mirror each other as arrogant and stubborn. If we talk about the improbable state of mind of the immigrants it is more than important to evoke the failure which constitutes the modern white French themselves.

Their fate was sealed as soon as they relied on the shoulder of the United States by the end of WWII. From that point, France had not only lost their status but also their independence. They would become the new colonized agents of the United States and Germany, later on, again. Such dependence would greatly contribute to the loss of French culture with the importation of the American way of life which happened gradually. The nation-state and nationalism, patriotism as a whole would be deemed archaic, racist, a thing of the past and above all, an anomaly in the globalist political agenda which is now becoming clearer and the unique future ahead of us. Though modern white French want to blame the immigrants for the issues of their country, they are the ones responsible for the demise of their own country. They never did anything to protect their heritage, unlike the Portuguese for example, and were arrogant enough to believe technological and economic progress to be their new identities. As they have now reached out a point where they are provided anything without having to work with the uberization of societies, they are now divided between lost patriots who are now strangers to their own customs and lost leftists who invent new causes, identities and pronouns as a reflection of their loss of identity too. Moreover, the model of French integration needs to be questioned. It is clearly obsolete and does not work anymore. The *grandeur* or a country does not only depend on the economic power of its institutions but also on the preservation of their culture and the dignity of the indigenous population. The reason why descendants of immigrants such as Assa Traoré destroy the nation from within and want to impose their new laws comes from the fact that the white French man does not scare anyone anymore. It would have been impossible for Traoré to do such things under Charles de Gaulle. It would be impossible to do it under Vladimir Putin, under Paul Kagame or even in Mali. Why? The population, proud of their heritage, would have never allowed her to tarnish the name of their institutions. Worst, Kagame or Putin, though different, scare people and deter foreigners from creating trouble. Assa Traoré is not a hero and is aware that the white French have failed to maintain their heritage. They do not scare anymore. Such results allow her to be arrogant towards them. On the contrary, other nations such as Albania or Croatia, though poorer than France could never tolerate such behavior. If poor, they never betrayed their heritage for technological development or money and they too had been mocked for it. Yet, their identity and dignity have been greatly preserved. There is now, no reason to hope or pray for France unless the great popular reset, a new revolution from the people occurs. Besides that, the nation will be remembered as the failure of the West.

CONCLUSION

The condition of black people in the west will probably end up tragically and turn into a political and social disaster. As we have said earlier, though they have been present in the West for sixty years for some, they have proven to have been economically and politically weak and useless. The mere existence and visibility of minorities in France and in the United States is due to their exploitation by the leftist side. They are dependent agents whose minds have already betrayed the African heritage for the sake of raw capitalism and its tactics. In the new global sphere, the fight for color has become obsolete. Indeed, since the end of the 1960s, most rebels in the United States and Africa have either been reduced to silence by death or sent to jail. After 1968 and the international youth movement against the values of the old world, sexual freedom was introduced in the prism of capitalism and the expansion of mercantilism to all spheres. From that point, the black community was no longer innocent as it was but aware of the calculative motivations behind their capitalistic protests. Therefore, just like any individual in the Western sphere, the diaspora has been tarnished by the toxicity of Western culture and has proven to be more loyal to money than to the preservation of their own essence. They not only massively consume but also buy and sell any ideology or concept which could seal their ego in the high popular demand of saviorism. That alone marks a tragedy and a great dysfunction of their state of mind especially when some communities, such as the Black French, had the opportunity to change and use their environement to become an example in the continent. The African descendants have become more and more arrogant and less efficient in many ways. Though exploited by the left, they are mostly resting on their laurels and fell into the friendly trap orchestrated by the white institutions. In this case, two *scenari* will likely happen for them. Indeed, as their condition will neither change nor evolve, the Western Blacks will either disappear or be annihilated by their institutions themselves. First, the propaganda of race-mixing will be used heavily to dilute their presence, a fact which could easily weaken their existence in the white sphere. In a century, France will no longer count fully black individuals among their ranks for most of them will be mixed to a certain degree. In the global political world these new members of the black community will have no religious, no cultural or any other deep attachment to Africa or Europe but will rather consider the capitalistic way of life to be theirs and a new expression of their culture. These lost mixed entities will be deprived of identities and will only be familiar to mass consumption, above all. Then, if proven not to be useful anymore by the left, the Blacks could be left alone. As they have been reluctant to change and work with humility on their social issues, they are now filled with anger, while they have not built anything at all. This brutality will not be forgiven by anyone and in order to fix the minds of the most rebellious among them, it is more than possible to see one given government send their army to annihilate or significantly reduce the angry black mobs. If the problems regarding the French ghettos do not change then the army could neutralize the most disruptive French Africans. One political turn could spark such a turmoil, especially if the far-right party, *Rassemblement National*, comes into office. This could be achieved by the end of the 2020 decade.

www.ingramcontent.com/pod-product-compliance
Lightning Source LLC
Chambersburg PA
CBHW070022260726
48658CB00011B/438